A FORMER LIFE

An overview of two centuries
60 years in the making

poems by

Bill Cushing

Finishing Line Press
Georgetown, Kentucky

A FORMER LIFE

An overview of two centuries
60 years in the making

ACKNOWLEDGMENTS

The listed titles first appeared in the following publications: *A Lullaby of Teeth*, anthology: "Alpha Dreams," "Final Flight," and "From California to Chicago;" *Altadena Poetry Review*, annual anthology: "Father's Day: June 20, 2004" and "Two Stairways;" *Borfski Press*: "Girl in Green;" *Brownstone Review*: "Drydocks and Parades;" *Getting Old*, anthology: "The Ancient Flocks of Wilson Street" and "With Dad;" *Glomag*: "Morning" and "Pelicans;" *Mayo Review*: "At a Mountain Waterfall," Blues for Earth," and "Recalling Their Smiles;" *Metaphor*: "Cusqueños;" *Onion River Review*: "Clarence;" *Over Land and Rising*, anthology, "Crossing a Rope Bridge;" *River Poets Journal Anthology*: "Sailing;" *Spectrum 3*: "What Love Is;" *Spectrum 10*: "Among the Wastes of Time;" "Easter Island in Koreatown;" *Stories of Music vol. 1*, anthology: "Music isn't about standing still and being safe;" *Stories of Music vol. 2*, anthology: "Listening to Bird;" *Sabal Palm Review*: "Fourth of July 1981," "Some Notes of a Religious Nature," and "Trash;" *The Song Is*: "On Modest Mussourgsky's 'Bydlo':' *West Trade Review*: "Pictures at Five."

Publisher: Leah Maines
Editor: Christen Kincaid
Cover Art: Marc Richards
Author Photo: Mari Cowen
Cover Design: Steven Rice (with Bill Cushing)

Printed in the USA on acid-free paper.
Order online: www.finishinglinepress.com
also available on amazon.com

Author inquiries and mail orders:
Finishing Line Press
P. O. Box 1626
Georgetown, Kentucky 40324
U. S. A.

Table of Contents

THINGS:

FOREWORD

I did not begin as a poet; actually, I was "late to the game" and did not get seriously involved in the art of writing poems until I was well past 30. In fact, the thought of writing had not even occurred to me then even though I always enjoyed both it and reading. So there are many people to thanks, and I suppose the first thanks should go to the people (whether known or not) and places that inspired the words contained in these pages. All my life's steps—the stumbles as well as (perhaps more than) the strides—provided what was needed to produce my poetry. However, there are some personal "thanks" warranted.

My first big "thank you" has to go to Deacon Kevin Bezner, my first English comp instructor at Florida Community College at Jacksonville (now Florida State College) after I finally decided to focus on my formal education. He saw potential worth encouraging, and I'm not alone as one who was influenced by his instruction and guidance. Along with Kevin, I should also mention Judy Elwell, wherever or however she may be, a longtime friend whose encouragement and pestering is most responsible for my do-over at formal education.

Still, there are others whose work and support (both literal and personal) helped create this volume.

My neighbors, Fabian and Carmen Marti, deserve kudos for encouraging and assisting me in my writing endeavors—even though not directly connected to the field.

Tom Moss has been a major part of my life for over 40 years, standing as my best man and godfather to our son; his feedback has always been appreciated if sometimes ignored, but he always had time to share with me.

Finally, I am in debt to Ghisela, my wife of 20-plus years, who has accommodated the demands I've made on her time, and I hope this publication is some repayment for that patience.

PEOPLE

A FORMER LIFE

I thought I saw John Fox today
riding the red Schwinn
it seemed he always had.
Then looking right, I saw a dog
that might have been Heidi
except it was a lab.

And stopping
for those seconds
on that street,
I waited
to smell
honeysuckle, but

the bike was quiet, lacking
clothes-pinned baseball cards
clattering against spokes;
then the ground the dog played on
returned to today, and
instantly, so did I.

PLANKING THE TANGO

Working with Harry, a Polish
carpenter with blunt fingers,
I spent my sixteenth summer
redecking the teak
of my father's forty-two footer,
a cutter built after World War II
ended and ended the line
of sailboats built by Owens.
We cut planks so dense
they destroy metal.
Bit by bit and blade by blade,
the acrid smoking steel
fills our nostrils
despite the Southerly
blowing off the Sound
each afternoon.

The wooden tongues
snuggled
into their grooves—
waiting for the black resin
to be spread: tar
so pervasive, so persistent
a presence
that only a monthly
buzz cut could get it
out of my hair,
and although
my father isn't always there
as I go through
each sweat-soaked day, it is the
closest I ever felt
to him.

TRASH

Out of early morning he comes
like a vendor peddling wares;
aluminum cans rattle
in the steel shopping cart
as he rattles along.

Scouring dumpsters
for twelve-ounce ore,
his time is spent
traveling streets
pitted with old
flip tops and discarded
cigarette butts:
fossils in asphalt.

Living with garbage,
the end result of civilization,
he collects society's castoffs
only to return them,
begin the cycle again.

CLARENCE

After a lifetime of farming,
tending land and animals,
you retired.

Replacing the rich smell of dung
with the moist scent of sawdust,
you took up hammer and chisel
to become a carpenter.
You said, half-joking,
it was the best way
to stay out from underfoot.
You told that to a reporter from Ames.

He wrote that should the Grim Reaper
ever knock on your door,
you'd invite him in for checkers
providing he was neither
a Democrat nor a Baptist;
after serving coffee,
playing a few games,
Death would probably leave,
a new customer.

Like many carpenters
you lost some fingers to your craft,
showing your heart
was in your work—
that sacrifice
being more important
than a few manual digits.

And the heart shows
in each finished product:
the wooden bowls
that came from a lightning-struck tree,
the clocks
all set seven minutes too slow,

or the stool
you built your great grandson:
the seat
heart-shaped,
the legs shortened
for smaller legs.

GIRL IN GREEN

Hair bobs around a face
of Nefertitian beauty:
She sits with an arm
draped over the arm
of a chair,
her green sleeve bends
from the stiff leaves
of a potted plant
shooting out of a clay urn.

Another sits, leaning
against the wicker, resting
her chin on a bended knee—
her eyes closed
and placid.

The girl in green
runs a hand
through the shoulder-length hair
of the other.

I feel that hand scratch
through my hair, the nails
separating greying ends,
the tips of her fingers
resting
as if on my skin.

My neck cranes at the touch.

AND BY ONE'S OWN HAND

People who drink
to solve their problems,
or feel better about them,
prove to themselves
that, no matter how bad
one feels, one can *always*
feel worse.

PICTURES AT FIVE

for D. K.

Kneeling on the floor,
thumbing through the albums
around me, I see
the pictures:
at five, on Santa's knee;
your first sailor's knot
in Cub Scouts;
tuxedoed for a prom. Then
you joined a different promenade,
one of brown and tattoos.
Now you bunk with
eight others in Ramadi.
Yesterday, Christmas Eve,
you called your mother and
me.

That's when I heard
of the insurgent
who came at you, pistol bared,
shooting, and you,
with your M16
"not readily available,"
grabbed your knife to spare
your life. These are
not the times
I wanted for my son,
so I went back to these old shots
and remembered those days
to avoid the images I now endure
until, God willing,
May.

THE ANCIENT FLOCKS OF WILSON STREET

They flock
to the park
cloaked in black,
perched on benches in the Winter sun,
the bills of their ball caps, like beaks,
dip in and out.

Like grackles
surrounding bread crumbs,
the ancient Armenians
ease their emotional baggage—
too young to remember
but old enough to recall those
who lived through
or died from
the Turkish carnage.
Surrounding the tables
filled with scattered dominoes,
on Christmas eve,
the old men chatter
about the old country
and its new destruction,
moving and
connecting
the ivory bones
with brittle fingers.

This little plot is now
their patch of earth,
and as
territorial
as the chastising mocking birds,
they chase strangers
        from the grounds,
children
        from weathered monkey bars.

RECALLING THEIR SMILES

being both a love and hate poem

Cancer has touched me
directly
four times,
losing a grandmother, a
wife, a
friend, and by way of my
sister, a brother in law.

Hendrike:
Before I was nine,
my grandmother died
from a distance
so that, by the time
I saw her,
       a stick figure under sheets
       holding a skull draped in
       parchment skin
       sprouting thin strands
       of stiff white hair,
I ran from the room,
insisting
she was not there.

Ana:
First she lost
a breast. Then,
when we thought
she was done,
I watched her
eaten alive, vomiting
the green mucous that was
her flowing out
       of her mouth
as she became less and less

the person she was.

William:
Resolute, a fighter wrapped in
a Romantic soul,
he hid his disease so well
that I didn't know of it
until
he told me
one night, between reps.
We enjoyed a last meal that
brought together all of our worlds
before he left his, this world,
two months later.

"We remember our friends
by their smiles,"
Tina said, recalling
William's unsmiling corpse,
that being what cancer
left for us.

Patrick:
Now I watch,
again from a distance,
waiting for the call I expect
but do not want

as my sister
approaches widowing
while her husband,
a man whose girth
built homes out of houses,
shrivels in size and prepares
to leave life,
three children, and my sister,

his wife.

My last image of the pair:
he stands next to
and bent over her,
her hair embraces his cheek
as he takes in her scent.

GABRIEL'S COMING

Things did not turn out
as perfectly as we had hoped. When
the doctors
extracted him
from the womb, there he was

a twisted pretzel of
a person, this child
who was
to be
perfect,

shaking and bloody
as a wounded bird and
not much different:

from the bony shoulders, like broken wings,
crooked arms splayed up
to the curled hands
that seemed jammed
under a quivering
chin
attached, haphazardly,
to a crooked head.

Hips
perpendicular to
a withered torso,
legs running
up the sides of a pruney chest—

all these deformities
from blood that had
clotted in the brain:
a stroke. So,
a malady
of the elderly became

his personal anomaly.

Blood soaked, crooked,
crying, and
brain damaged:

this was how we greeted
our son,
yet
from those bodily barricades
and
out of that
unquenchable panic
came
a boy who
        did not interrupt a family,
        did not join a family,
but who
created a family.

FATHER'S DAY: June 20, 2004

I watched my mother die over days:
Eyes sealed shut, glazed
with a crust of time;
occasional sounds pantomiming
conversation; breathing
barely there and marked
with wearied effort.
Hands sprout
from two thin and shriveled
arms, laying
wherever placed; her legs,
scabbed from the falls
of her last
conscious moments.

My father, the martial stoic,
sits beside her,
leans into her, and
whispers in her ear,
"It's okay to go
if you wish," telling her,
"I'm ready."
In a half-century
of life,
I had never seen
such tenderness:
his age-mottled hands stroke
shallow cheeks,
a half-finger
brushes back brittle hair,

and while it took three days to complete—
on this Father's Day, my father inclined
to give my mother
the gift of dying.

WHAT LOVE IS

We don't see the twists and bends in the road
of life as we make our blind way, yet still
when we're there, we learn to shoulder its load.
I found I didn't know real love until
I was bound to raise a broken child.
who was given this, not a life he chose.
Seeing him in bed, I am reconciled
to arms and legs forming a sprinter's pose,
splayed in action never to be taken:
a serene child who will never know
romantic affection yet will take in
sincere love he will spread and cause to grow.
The lump in my throat is not some tumor.
It's the prying pulse of my heart's tremor.

WITH DAD

Gone and now cremated,
I wait for my sister
to meet me at his now-
once bungalow. Searching
through the remains,
sifting among clothes
he left behind,

I put on a jacket
hanging in the closet,
turn toward the mirror
on an opposing wall.
I see gray hair and a beard,
half a century old,
but below that,

the jacket swallows
the child: its shoulders end
at my biceps; the cuffs
of each sleeve brush
against my knuckles.
Blushing, I remove the coat,
turn back to the closet, and

return it to its rightful place.

SUICIDE NOTES

John

Sitting rakishly,
blonde hair, bright eyes,
a cigarette cradled between
fingers resting on fading jeans.
In the right hand, a pen,
his best weapon
against the world.
And underneath the words:
       "He died,
       a victim of suicide,
       in March 1990."
Ah, suicide,
the ultimate gangster act:
a scene in which criminal
and victim
are one and the same.

Unnamed

Barechested, he looks off the page
with drooping eyes, angelic and sad,
and the looks
of a movie star
posing for a poster. Yet,
the story goes,
he was found in the hotel bed, fetal,
with a single round, hollow-point .38,
in the chamber. He held
the police at bay
seven and one-half hours—
almost a full working day,
a transient locked in a hotel wing.
The note in the can
relayed implications,
but answered no questions.

Allison

Old enough for anguish,
yet too young to see
other options. How easy,
sometimes, to forget
life's most difficult choices
are often the best,
but the choice is yours.
Life may be boring, terrifying, or trite,
but, above all, one must stay alive.
Hardest job on earth.

MORNING

Is
my favorite time of day:

Waking to an aroma of mangoes,
your scent;
feeling the weightlessness
of curly hair;
I can hear the easy
rise of breath;
a sculpted
cheek and chin
rest on
my right shoulder
while the thumb and
forefinger of my left palm
lay flat, forming
a "v" along
a smooth cheek.

Then, in a manner that would humble
Helen of Troy herself,
you rise,
languid and liquid,
and the lunar glow
of your cool body
moves into the light, casting
a crescent shadow
around your breast, your hips.

Then your face
turns toward me
and a smile spreads to
greet the day.

Then,
I rise with you.

PLACES

IN PINK NEON

Chrome and black tile at breakfast again;
coffee's so strong it pulls your eyelids back
going down, and while last evening's drunks,
with five a.m. shadows, use it
to try to face the new day,
women, legs on spiked heels, lift leather skirts
to reveal specialties of the house—
initiating a physical negotiation,
trading the tangible
for currency.

In closed cuffed hand, scalene triangle
of whole wheat drips from sunnyside-up.
A single waitress covers ground.
Butter, warmed by sun shining through slatted glass,
slowly rolls down a stack of browned pancakes;
silverware clatters, china
against china; napkin falls;
voices chatter—while outside, in pink neon,
a sign glows: "Best Food in Town."
And it is.

DRYDOCKS AND PARADES

The warm breezes of great heights
ran through fine
light hair
as I straddled
my father's neck,
gripping tight to his collar
as veterans marched proudly by:
Ike's years then.

Days of wonderful dizziness,
looking at
that parade of men below me:

a fearful pleasure—like now,
climbing kingposts
and stanchions
of eighty-thousand ton tankers
built with half-inch steel
and starplate from the keel up —
using cables, rivets, bolts,
torches, and welds.

CROSSING A ROPE BRIDGE

Coaxing myself to place a foot on
that hesitant first step
of the crossing, a journey with outcome
neither known nor guaranteed.
Isolation is a very shaky place
where circles of behavior echo
or resolve into a hydra or, worse,
demons of solitude.

Stopping on this wobbly avenue,
my feet feel vibrations deep in their soles,
and I wonder: Where is the tipping point?

Peeking down to see a drop deeper
than that uncertain climb
to the other side, to the safe haven
of the forest veiled in mist.
Then vertigo, fear of failure, overwhelms
so that retreating into the numb
appears an easier alternative
to taming the dragon.

EASTER ISLAND IN KOREATOWN

Sitting
on a gallon paint can
delivering
a weird brand
of royalty to the curb
of Vermont Avenue,
his square face, brown:

a cross
between some ancient
pharaoh
and a gargoyle;
his hands, rest
on blue-jeaned knees,
fingers pointed down.

Meanwhile,
traveling south, bungeed
secure
in the back
of a flatbed truck,
a laughing Buddha stands.
He signals "touchdown"

while passing
a neighborhood bar
and grill, where,
from the window,
a neon sign
proclaims,
"Natural light."

CHÂTEAU FORTE LA RIVIÉRE CHER

Paying the Loire tribute,
Cher rises in the northwest,
then flows across a plateau
to join the Yevre at Vierzon.

Eighteenth century masons
built the chateau from, and on,
pilings of a sixteenth-
century mill, creating

a castle more squat than wide.
Torch-lit halls linked galleries,
ballrooms, the castle fastened
riverbanks with black-and-white tiles,

witness to minuets, waltzes. Then,
pawns crossed this checkerboard that
was then scuffed by the jackboots
of soldiers of the thousand-year Reich

lasting only twelve — a fraction
of the fuehrer's promises.
Taking flight from Gothic weight,
the structure offered flight

to its builder's descendants.
They had no way of knowing,
these workmen who joined shores with
stone, the path they left. Placing

this architectural bridge
on arched columns, they spanned
generations both backward
and forward. They did not see

events that were to be yet
still supplied an avenue

to freedom for their great-
grandchildren's grandchildren.

AMONG THE WASTES OF TIME

1978

Stumbling through hallways muttering,
she pokes a cane in corners, asking,
    "What's that?
    Who's there?"
to empty air.
She's become an inconsistent mind
in an incontinent body. Later,

lying on a bed shielding
hidden cans and dry goods
she herself has forgotten are there,
she whimpers, calling
the name
of her older brother, a man
who in thirty years
has heard nothing.

1986

In an old building an old man, a retired major,
shits in his pants and curses
the insubordinate body that refuses,
anymore, to obey and does as it pleases
when it pleases
in a manner which would shame God Himself.

Later, visiting his wife, two decades dead,
he shakes and frets
on the bench,
surrounded by the tombstones that
protrude from the ground
like fingertips of the buried
fighting to claw their way free of the earth.

CUSQUEÑOS

Up where the mountains
curl like sleeping dragons,
peaks piercing
far above the clouds,
in another world
two miles
above sea level sits
the center of the Incan empire,
Cusco: a *pupute*,
bellybutton of the world.

Like a crouching panther
this place,
all diagonal
slopes, everything
hard stone: boulders, smooth squares
of grey granite the size
of a room; cobblestones,
loose ovals of softer pastels;
and of course, interrupting
the landscape is the weighted
masonry of churches with arches
lifting statues
promising spirituality
but instead
delivering conquest.

In the morning comes
the hammering from the town square:
a stonemason crouches amid
rocks, boulders, and stones.
His song rings out
with each ping of the steel
striking the rock
he works on. Not far,
the finisher chips
discretely on the rough work,

trimming the rock into shapes
that could easily
have come from a lathe.

Then there are the people,
the *cusqueños:*
Trudging along
the sloping roads and paths,
they carry belongings
or wares in the *liclla—*
colorful blankets sprouting
babies, flowers, hay,
or more stones,
the wraps that
wrap
around stooping shoulders
and seem to push the carriers
into their own incline
as they make their shuffling way
up these narrow and steep
streets while we tourists steep
coca tea in our rooms,
attempting to adjust
to the heights.

At midnight
we bolt awake, our bodies
gulping air to catch breath; feeling
a tingling in fingers,
we drown in thin air.

The *cusqueños,*
like the stones surrounding them,
are squat, browned,
with hearts enlarged
and noses slightly widened:
equipment for the altitude.

The old ones peer
through occidental eyes
cracked and peeling
from age and
knowledge,
knowledge ancient
and pure.

The look says,
"*Nokanchis ocmanta causanchis:*"
we will endure."

WASHINGTON STREET

It is always, it seems, an inner-city street:
lined with warehouses accentuated
by cinderblock projects too concrete
to induce dreams.

Purple-painted cement patios
seem to bend under maroon velour couches
filled with larger-than-life women
fanning bandanna-wrapped faces while

their thin men huddle around tables
drinking beer out of cans and
playing cards for chump change.
A bus grumbles along

mixing diesel fumes with the exhaust
of crack. Inside, a blue-tattooed
ex-con tries seducing a girl in the seat nearby.
She talks of Jesus, the afterlife,

and her church. He promises to meet her there—
although their "theres" are at odds. Still,
he prays for what might happen after dark
in a consecrated park

off Washington Street.

TWO STAIRWAYS

The first greets guests as they parade
through the foyer to a sunken living room.
The steps—wide with carpeted tread—
ease along gilded walls

interrupted only by staid portraits
of patriarchs. Lips brush cheeks,
besitos de cultura alto,
as the gathering, elegant guests

follow the living room
past a massive dining room table
where innocuous ceramic buttons,
doorbell fixtures strategically placed

to summon the help from the kitchen
that hides the second staircase: steep, jagged,
and above all concrete. Servants—
with rough hands wrapped in skin

darker than the mahogany furniture
they rub to a high shine—
trudge between floors carrying meals,
laundry, lemon water,

and imperceptible curses
triggered by the buzzing commands.
Worms of rage burrow
Deep into their hearts.

AFTER EL NIÑO: February 24, 1998

for Lynne Cohn, who left town one day too soon

A foamy surf of clouds breaks
over the San Gabriel mountains
becoming what you had hoped to find.
El niño has, for the moment, left,
and finally, today, it is
sunny Southern California.

Wildflowers, shining and purpled,
highlight the green valleys unlike
the veil of yesterday's sheets
of rain and clouds, heavily
folded slate-grey brush strokes. Now,
white-veined and dusted with snow,

the peaks of the valley ridges curve
beside the freeway, and a ribbon of light
runs red along their arched backs
while evening sets and the sun stacks
blankets of pinks and greenish blues
over brown-and-burnt hues.

AT A MOUNTAIN WATERFALL

water slaps
my face
forcing my eyes
shut
as we climb
      crablike
              scuttling
      platform
           to platform
     along the rocks
that form   an opening
not more than   a half-foot across
           and
from that six-inch
      aperture
           water
           shoots
                out
                and
                down
    rocks
    run
    in steps
         handholds
some jut out with
holes   in them

vines crawl
down
and—nourished by
     water that
splashes
     runs
pounds
     and
flows—
begin to

take root
as they

touch
down
on
another base of rock

holding a stone
shaped
like an ax
blade
as big
as my hand
and as thick
and
almost as flat
except for one
hard wart at
the broader end

other men
might have been
here using rocks
like this one
chipping them into tools
and weapons

this island
reminds one
of all things
primitive

FROM CALIFORNIA TO CHICAGO

The rolling surf and mists of
clouds reflect
the sunlight
off the side of our flight
and into the Grand Canyon:
three rock formations snake
through the gigantic gullet,
their peaks like the spine
of an iguana.

The inverted capillaries,
veins, and arteries of
river beds cut through
the landscape,
indentations that seem as if
God had scraped spoons
of ice cream
out of the earth.

The topography transforms
into faces in the terrain,
and we look down on contortions
of grimaces.

Landing, we slide beneath
the bellies of arriving
and departing jets.
"The moving walkway is now
ending; please look down."
Above, candy colored
coat hangers of neon
burn and cool the area while
rising up into the concourse
of O'Hare, a plastic and chrome
Grand Central Station
for the new millennium,
opening floodgates

for the art of denial,
washing away
all silt of tradition.

THINGS

LISTENING TO BIRD

Flying through scales
he did the impossible, stretching

staccato sounds,
stopping only to change direction.

He found places
in his search for every note

not imagined:
leaving chromatic gravity,

breaking confines,
shooting up into infinity;

then he rested,
hanging on a single, random chord;

bending branches
of music (but never breaking them),

lingering
wherever he chose, staying

just long enough
to make it his territory

and his alone.

ALPHA DREAMS

The wolf bares fangs
even when sleeping.

Legs move
in rapid dream-twitches;
cheeks quiver from tickling
branches that swipe his head.

Leading the hunt,
he chases with others of the pack—
      sweaty fear
      fills his nostrils
      and sanguine expectation
      tingles through his thighs.
Nipping,
then ripping
at the flanks of a deer,
they jump
with him, as one.
Then, the imagined pack
straddles its fallen meal,
dining
without grace.

A lullaby of teeth,
as enamel scrapes against bone,
and the song of sinew,
stretching before tearing free from
the cooling carcass,
fill his night.

SAILING

for Joseph Conrad

I have always taken
the four a.m. watch:
those three hours before dawn when,
inhaling the moist sweetness
of a new day, we awake
and escape last night's darkness,

leaving technology
to experience
quiet and primitive satisfaction.

The ocean rushing underneath,
its volume
dependent upon current hull speed,
spills a phosphorescent wake —
the only natural source of light
besides the moon.

Rolling up and down,
swaying into balance
on the balls of my feet while
cradling the warmth
of a mug's contents.

Soon
an orange sliver appears
and grows, as the sun
finds the seam in the weld
that fixes sea to sky.

PELICANS

Slowly circling,
the pelican

drops like a stone
into water.

Then climbing the
air, he stops, and

with a single
motion of wings,

glides on the wind.

ON MODEST MUSSOURGSKY'S "BYDLO"

A shape appears
and is gone,
comes into view,
disappears, until,
cresting the hill,
the spot
blotting the sun,
a cartload of hay,
takes shape.

Emerging,
the wagon,
oxen-drawn, a juggernaut pulled
by two thousand pounds,
rolls between fields—
grinding dirt,
crushing stones.

Sweating flanks
of coarse,
matted hair
cause slow,
rhythmic hammering,
dull thunder
as hooves pound earth.
The ground moves
to the sound
of these hardened
timpani.

Beast and wagon pass,
processional,
as if solemn,
and then recede
slowly
out of sight.

A wake is left—
strong pungent odor
of musk
mixed
with the sweet sharpness
of the cut stalks
being carried
to the village beyond.

TURNING FIFTY

If you've done life right
you do not feel or even
see the years coming
until they have long passed.

One day you look down
and see the hands
of an older man:
gnarled, blunt, corded

with venular ropes of age.
The lines on the face
in the mirror seem
as if they have been there

always.

Now you understand
how far the distance
from the start actually is.

The body has not yet betrayed,
but it's well on its way,
and you know that

the fight has begun.

"Music isn't about standing still and being safe."

Miles Davis (1926 - 1991)

listen

two weeks after you died
a quarter-million thronged
by the St. Johns River
to hear the music you had spawned
hoping to see you
but
even in death
you never looked back

they were all there
        Hannibal   Bird
        Chick   Jo-Jo
        Red   Jaco
        Bean   Dizzy
        my favorite   Freddie Freeloader

isolated
you
        were a beacon
        a flagship for messages
                of the heart

back to the crowd   unbowed
that proud dance-walk
announced by muted horn
that spoke
and broke
through all the bull
and told us about a place

Miles

ahead of everyone else

50

you spent a lifetime
         thinking for yourself
         speaking to every generation
playing it all:

         jazz   blues
         funk   rock
         fusion
categories took
a backseat
to creativity
         and rhythm

                  space

         and feeling
                  spirit

I remember fourth grade
picking up a horn
then laying it down
rock and roll was my world
what did I know

seven years later I heard

it was in the Garden
where you brought me back
to music

I walked all the way home

Miles

from that train station
my head pounding with sounds
frantic-fast as the subway

I spent the night on
          those African rhythms
          you used decades
          before anyone else
even thought to
filling my head
letting me know
I'd have it all down cold
if I could walk
as cool as the notes you heard
          coming from

Miles

you had that thing
          that style
that spark that was
a blue flame
          jumping
          off a gas stove
igniting everything   everywhere
touching the genetic
resonant
frequency
in all

BLUES FOR EARTH

April 22, 1990: Jacksonville, Florida

To alter nature we build
build bridges   sidewalks
structures
doing our damnedest
to undo
the rolling wonder
of this planet
we deny ourselves
nature

all bureaucratic efforts
amount to litter
all our rubbish
should be outlawed
as a crime against God
       or Nature
       or Whatever
       or Whichever
       or Whomever
is responsible for this planet

even billboards and highways
should be dismantled

look around anywhere
       everywhere
       we're cutting into the earth
       co-ordinating
straight lines   constructing
corners   conforming us
all right angles
boxing us in   boring us
placing
everyone into categories
       consumer

                provider
                predator

        peak of the food chain

        perhaps the really intelligent animals
        traded in opposable thumbs
        for fins
                    dew claws

SOME NOTES OF A RELIGIOUS NATURE

Jesus was sent
to die for our sins
like some package
from UPS.

He delivered the goods
to humanity
and we delivered him
back to Heaven

battered, beaten,
mutilated.
Some creation
we turned out to be.

MARCH 9, 2009: Fifty years on

Even though
she's fifty now,
I'm blamin' Barbie
anyhow.
She still titillates;
she's the reason I seek
long legs,
mountain peaks
of breasts, and high cheeks.
I have seen
her parts piled
in mounds
in the backyard,
yet male eyes still
follow every
outlandish curve
of her still
but smooth body:
Bright blonde hair flowing
over supernaturally
proportioned hips and smooth
but crooked arms. Besides,
how can men be faithful
to one when
there are
so many of her?
Doctors, lawyers,
surfers, executives,
models, and now
even inked, like
the ultimate
biker chick.

ECCE HOMO

Upon viewing "The Ascension of Christ"

Lips partially open,
Jesus begs for us.
Looking up through tears of blood,
the eyes shimmer
with the pain of his position.

One foot rests on the planet
while he rises, just
barely,
struggling up
out of this
niche in the rock
in a chamber in Cusco's
el Convento de Santa Catalina.

Conceived and left
by an unknown artist
of the seventeenth century,
Christ looks already bowed
by the task
of carrying our sins
on sagging shoulders.
Below him,
on earth, Adam
covers himself
as he takes the fruit;

there is no sign of the serpent.

Meanwhile,
the sisters of the order
take communion behind curtains,
separated from
and unseen by
the congregation.
This is their world.

APOLOGIA

First commandment: "Thou shalt have no other gods before me."

I,
a fallen spirit,
made a forced exit;
ultimate love for Him
led to this downfall, this
condition of torment
I now lead.

Heaven,
then,
was ageless, changeless,
forever and eternal—
as I was.

Still am.

The law was laid down ages before
man, before
altars, before
temples or churches, before the writing of
law itself. Then,
that First Commandment was altered and
given to mankind: trivial creatures
created out of ego,
then possessed by it. It is ego,
not knowledge,
that is original sin.

Remember this:
before you were, that command stood
for all—animals, plants,
even angels,
but when clay and dust
were mixed
with the breath of life

to become an imposter
of their creator,
then
even angels were told,

"Kneel before men."

Now,
my temptations serve as testimony
to man's worthlessness,
proving his Bible and God's own words
correct.

The torture of souls is only
an afterthought, only
reciprocity of torment.

For my refusal to bow,
I suffer now;

as do you.

FOURTH OF JULY 1981

Clouds, like a herd of whales,
dark bellies passing overhead,
wheel and turn, moving northeast.

I stand beneath that majestic entourage
watching, at dusk on the Fourth of July,
while the children down the street stop

lighting Roman candles, running
to seek the shelter of porch roofs
as Nature's fireworks outdo Man's.

TO A MOTHER, ON THE 2,025th BIRTHDAY OF HER SON

What was it like, Mary, laying
on a rough and rank bed of straw
waiting for the final push, then
the newborn? There were no stirrups

save those that might have hung across
a wooden crossbeam left by some
anonymous traveler, safe
and warm in a bed in the inn.

Was delivery more trying,
giving birth with an unbroken
hymen? Did you get to compare
this birth to any others? What

was it like, Mary, inhaling
the thick stench of the placenta
while you were holding your newborn
child, only to learn later that,

no matter how miraculous
this particular conception,
your son's fate would ultimately
be a blood-soaked death.

FINAL FLIGHT

I slept through those initial collisions,
the twin explosions
as steel and fuel met concrete and girder
for the final collapse
into rock and powder of two towers
meant as monuments
to the grandeur of their century.

I saw it from a safe distance—
not living through events
except for my own recall. I can
still note those, retrieve
the day, but the singular image
I cannot shed, the one
that refuses to leave my head is that

of those people, the 200 left who,
facing the option
of burning alive, knowing at that moment
they were indeed dead,
chose instead, like Icarus,
to spread their arms
in almost-welcome embrace of

the quarter-mile journey back to earth.

Named in honor of a Civil War Navy hero, **Bill Cushing** has lived in Virginia, New York, Pennsylvania, Missouri, Florida, Maryland, the Virgin Islands, and Puerto Rico before moving to California. As an undergrad, he was called the "blue collar" poet by classmates at the University of Central Florida because of his years in the Navy and later working as an electrician on oil tankers, naval vessels, and fishing boats before he returned to college at the age of 37. He earned an MFA in writing from Goddard College in Vermont and teaches at East Los Angeles and Mt. San Antonio colleges, residing in Glendale with his wife and their son.

As a writer, Bill has been published in various literary journals, magazines, and newspapers, including *The San Juan Star* and the *Florida Times-Union*. His short stories have appeared in *Borfski Press, Newtown Literary Journal* and *Sediments*. His creative non-fiction piece "A Father's Pride" was a finalist in 2016's Pen 2 Paper competition for writings concerning the disabled.

He had poems in both issues of the award-winning *Stories of Music*, among other anthologies. A Pushcart Prize nominee, Bill was named as one of the Top Ten Poets of L.A. in 2017, and his work was featured in a collection of regional poets by Moon Tide Press in an anthology named *Lullaby of Teeth*, a title that came from a line in one of his poems. He also has a poem featured in a textbook focused on Los Angeles for area high school students. His poetry has appeared in numerous journals, both in print and online, including *Avocet, Brownstone Review, Glomag, Mayo Review, Penumbra, Poetry Nook, Spectrum, The Song Is. . .,* and *West Trade Review*.

When not teaching or writing, Bill facilitates a writing workshop in Eagle Rock, California (9 Bridges). He also performs with a musician in a project called "Notes and Letters." He invites anyone interested to visit and "like" their Facebook page or check their youtube page, "Chuck Corbisiero Bill Cushing Notes and Letters."

www.ingramcontent.com/pod-product-compliance
Lightning Source LLC
Chambersburg PA
CBHW021200090426
42740CB00008B/1168